AF481293
Kids should always be
respectful and polite.

Parents should be kind,
caring and never fight.

Employees should work hard and not be lazy.

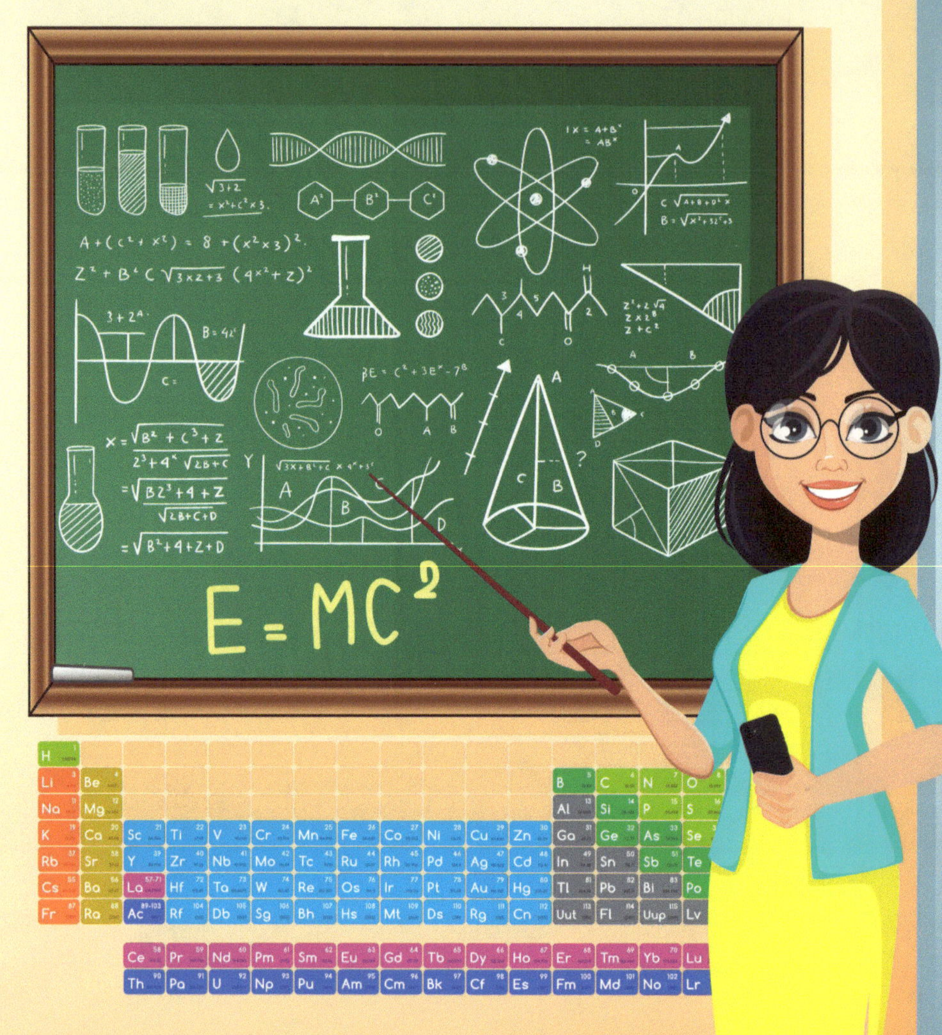

Teachers should be intelligent and tech savvy.

Animals should be playful
and not messy.

Restaurant servers should be
fast and not fussy.

Mechanics should be honest and
not lie to increase profits.

Plumbers should not overcharge
for jobs they do in minutes.

Dentists should not drill holes in perfectly fine teeth unnecessarily.

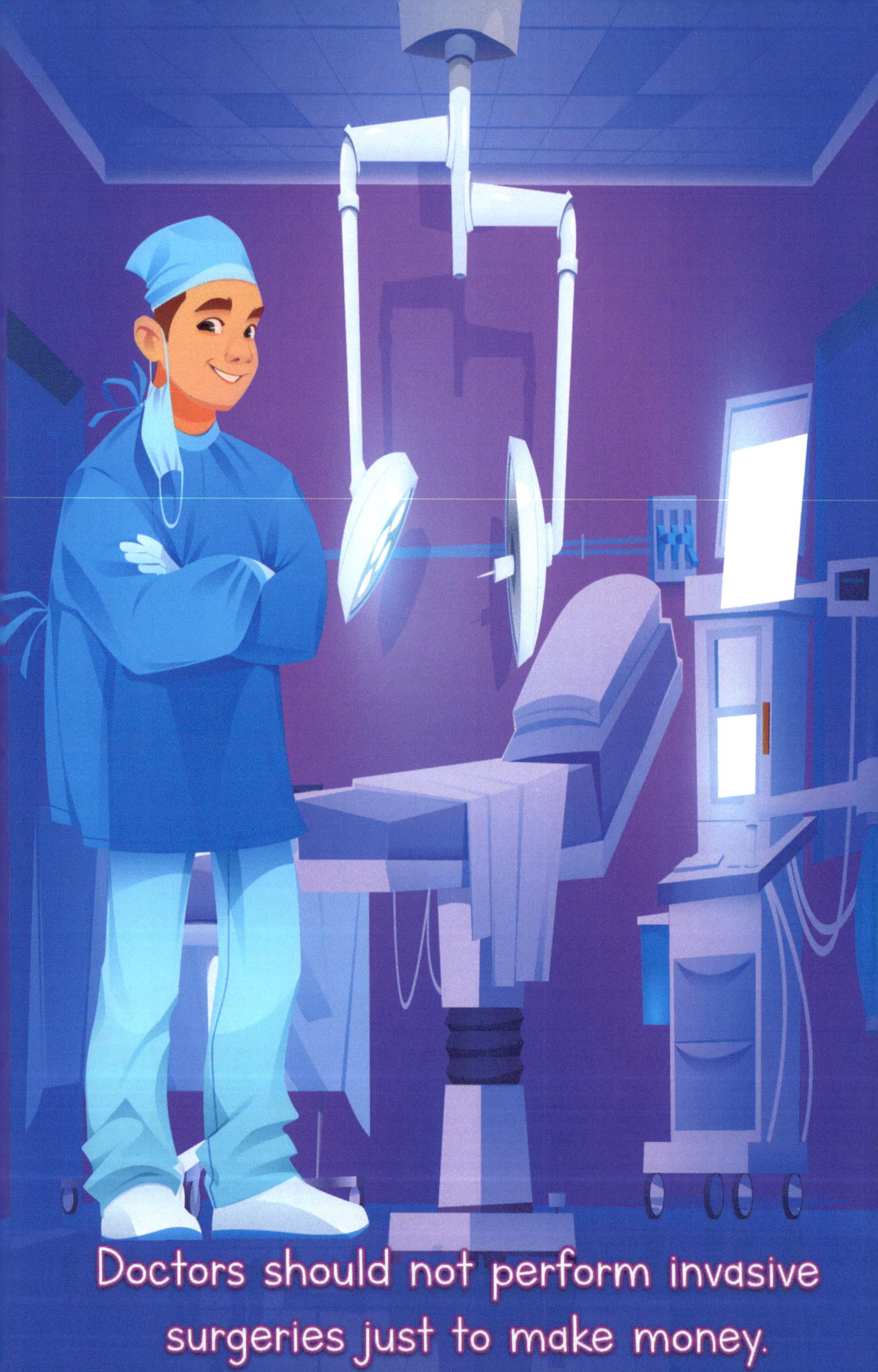

Doctors should not perform invasive surgeries just to make money.

Comedians should not offend some people to make others laugh.

Real estate brokers should pay commissions for referrals, or cut their fees in half.

Football quarterbacks should know
how to scramble, pass and not get sacked.

Coaches should yell and agonize less so they don't prematurely have a heart attack.

Web designers should eliminate viruses, malware and build user friendly websites.
VIRUS

Boys and men should not wear pants that are so uncomfortable, revealing and tight.

Politicians should be ethical, moral and truly serve the people who elect them.

Teenagers should be obedient to parents,
cause less trouble and mayhem.

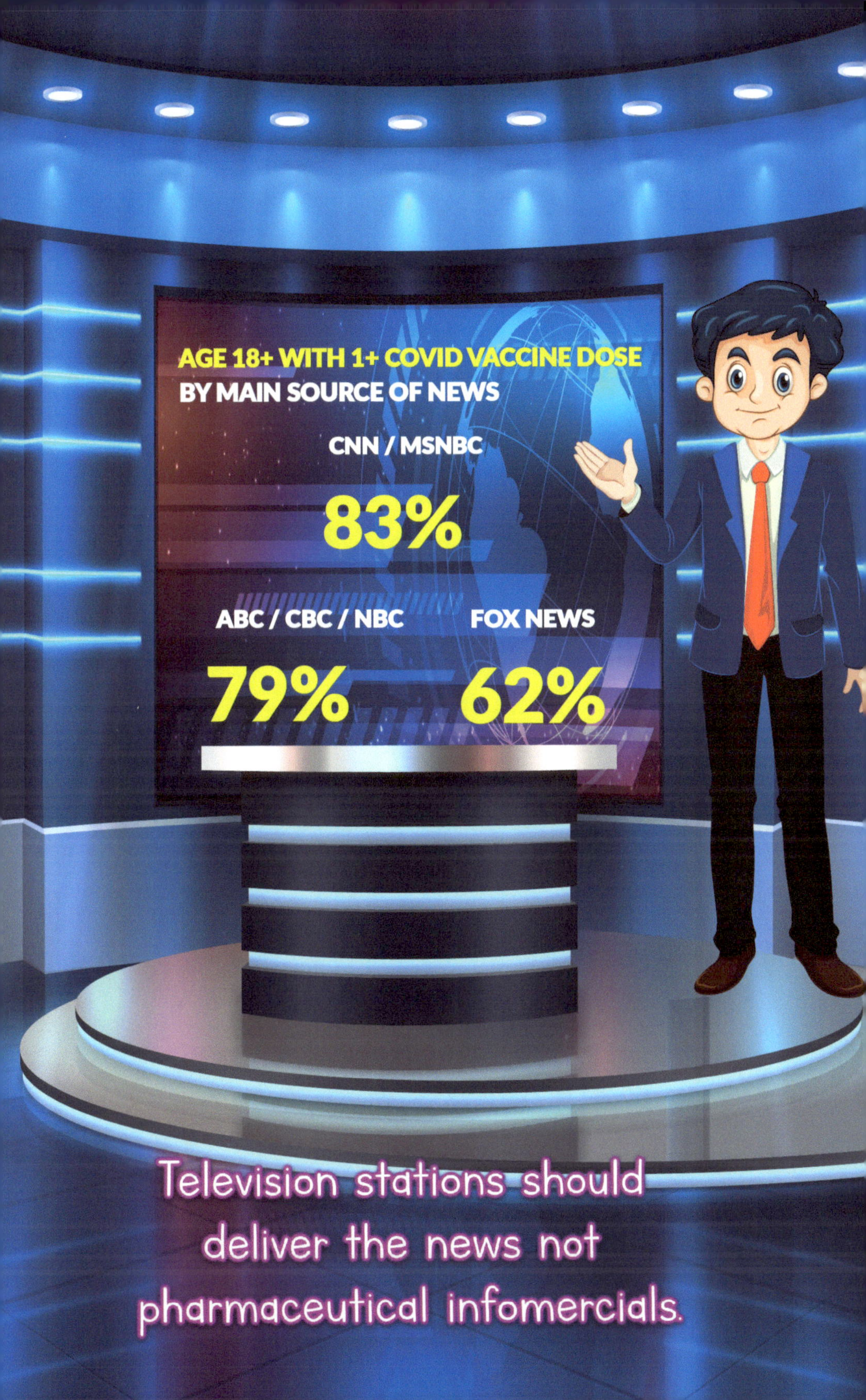

AGE 18+ WITH 1+ COVID VACCINE DOSE
BY MAIN SOURCE OF NEWS
CNN / MSNBC
83%
ABC / CBC / NBC
79%
FOX NEWS
62%
Television stations should deliver the news not pharmaceutical infomercials.

Journalists should be more well read, truthful, less partisan and emotional.

Much to repair
Much to restore
Much to heal
Presidents should understand policy,
not have dementia,
nor read from a teleprompter.

Governments should put their people's interests before grabbing for themselves dollars.

Children's book writers should focus on more fun, whimsical and lighthearted topics.

Vacations should happen
closer to the equator,
far away from snow, near the tropics.

Publishers and literary agents should consider unknown authors who are awesome.

Students should not be allowed
to have phones in school,
lest they be distracted and remain dumb.

GEOMETRY

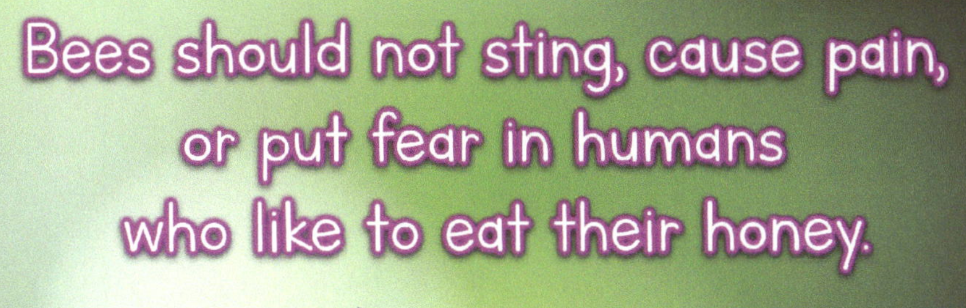

Bees should not sting, cause pain,
or put fear in humans
who like to eat their honey.

Daily life and personal happiness
should not be so restricted
and limited by money.

Salesmen, business owners and entrepreneurs should be confident, not rude and bold.

The currencies of the world
should not fluctuate so wildly
and be more stable like gold.

When things don't go your way,
stop SHOULD-ing everywhere
and forget the past.

Be aware and discerning, but don't agonize
because most challenges in life
come, go and do not last.

START

Happy cartoons should not
be coupled with commercial products
for kids to be sold.

Salty
BRAND
NATURAL INGREDIENTS
CHIPS

toys for
kids
a toy shop

Children should obediently bathe,
brush their teeth and go to bed
promptly when they are told.

All people should kneel, thank God
and pray before bed
and to begin each new day.

Do so for your problems to decrease,
blessings increase and God
to show you the way.

9 798423 648435